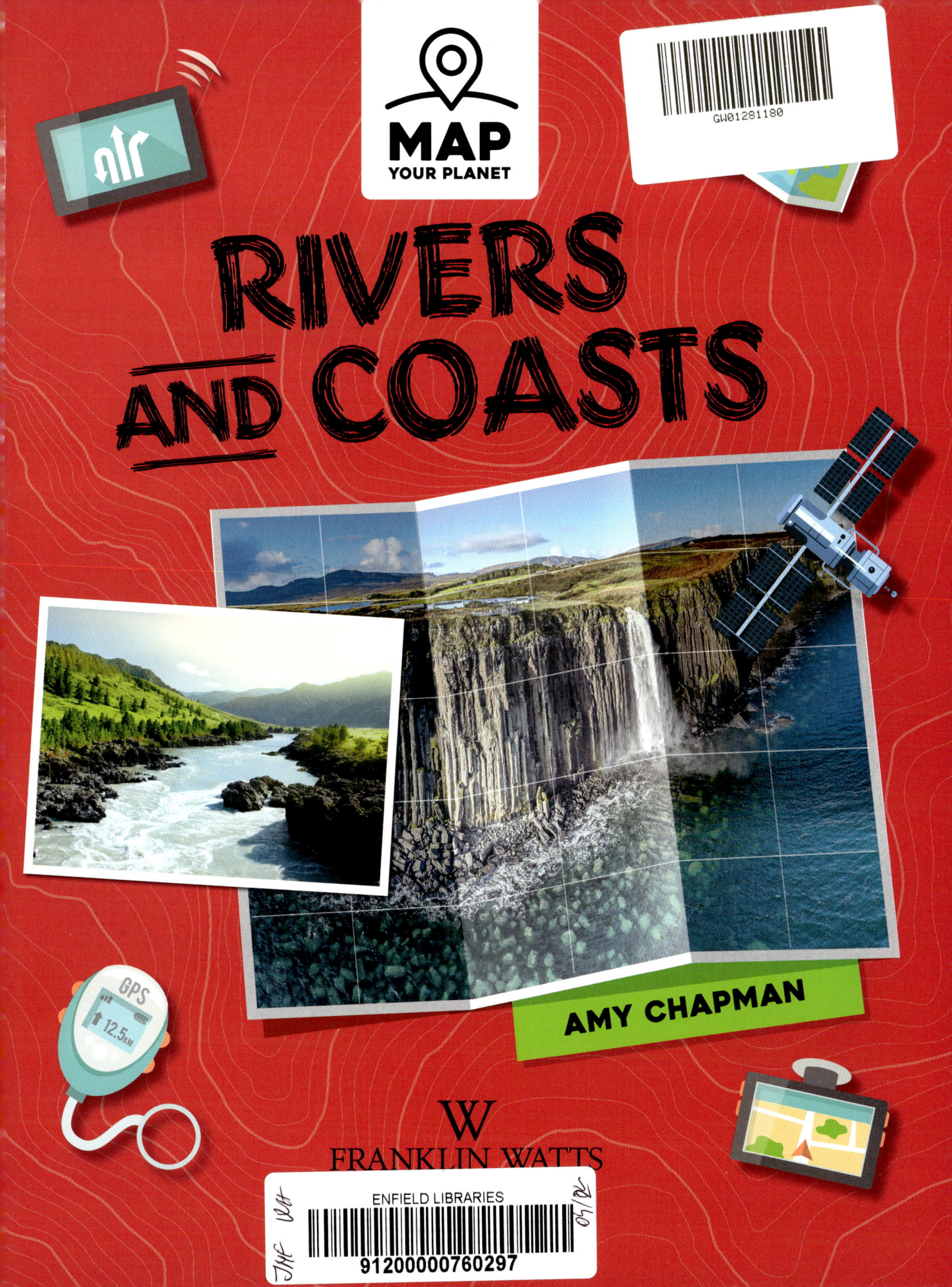

RIVERS AND COASTS

MAP YOUR PLANET

AMY CHAPMAN

FRANKLIN WATTS

Franklin Watts

First published in Great Britain in 2021 by the Watts Publishing Group

Copyright © the Watts Publishing Group 2021

Produced for Franklin Watts by
White-Thomson Publishing Ltd
www.wtpub.co.uk

All right reserved

Series editor: Izzi Howell
Series designer: Rocket Design (East Anglia) Ltd

HB ISBN 978 1 4451 7324 5
PB ISBN 978 1 4451 7325 2

The publisher would like to thank the following for permission to reproduce their pictures:
Alamy: FLHC MAPS '9' 21(c); Getty: sushi7688 5, SusanneSchulz 10(t), Jim desant 747 14(b), Universal History Archive/Universal Images Group 20(c), jejim 28(c); NASA: 15(t); Shutterstock: Sergey Dzyuba 4(c), wickerwood 4(b), Mushakesa 5(t), Jay Stuhlmiller 6(c), corbac40 6(b), Aleksey Sagitov 7, Matyas Rehak 8, Daniel Prudek 9(t), Jonathan Chancasana 9(b), mapichai 10(b), Sander Claes 11(t), Merkushev Vasiliy 11(b), Malgorzata Litkowska 13(t), Egyptian Studio 16, Egyptian Studio 17(t), agsaz 17(b), Tum-Cruise 18(c), VectorMine 18(b), shutterupeire 19(t), Modulo19(b), Gparker 22(b), VectorMine 23(t), Mariusz Hajdarowicz 23(b), Natali Snailcat 23(c), Kirstudiofilms 24(b), siete_vidas 25(c), JB Manning 25(b), Travel mania 26(b), snapgalleria 27(t), Francois BOIZOT 27(b), jejim 28, jejim 29(t), burakyalcin 29(b); USGS: 13(b).

Design elements by Shutterstock

Map illustrations: Julian Baker: 12–13, 16–17, 24–25, 28–29; Techtype: 8–9

Every effort has been made to clear copyright. Should there be any inadvertent omission, please apply to the publisher for rectification.

The website addresses (URLs) included in this book were valid at the time of going to press. However, it is possible that contents or addresses may have changed since the publication of this book. No responsibility for any such changes can be accepted by either the author or the publisher.

All facts and statistics were correct at the time of press.

Printed in Dubai

Franklin Watts
An imprint of
Hachette Children's Group,
Part of the Watts Publishing Group
Carmelite House
50 Victoria Embankment
London EC4Y 0DZ

An Hachette UK Company
www.hachettechildrens.co.uk

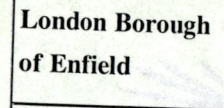

London Borough of Enfield	
91200000760297	
Askews & Holts	15-Mar-2022
J910.9169 JUNIOR NON	
ENWINC	

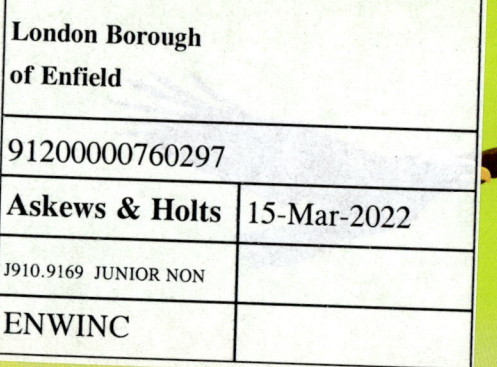

CONTENTS

Rivers and coasts 4
A river's source 6
📍 Mapping the Amazon River 8
The upper and middle courses 10
📍 Mapping the Kentucky Bend 12
Reaching the sea 14
📍 Mapping the Nile Delta 16
Types of coast 18
📍 Mapping new shores 20
Coastal changes 22
📍 Mapping La Manga 24
Using water 26
📍 Mapping the Three Gorges Dam 28
Glossary 30
Further information 31
Index 32

RIVERS AND COASTS

A river is a long stretch of freshwater that flows across the land. A coast is a place where land meets an area of saltwater, such as the ocean. We can see both of these features on maps.

CHANGING THE LANDSCAPE

The movement of water along rivers and coastlines shapes the landscape in many ways. Rivers carve out valleys and form curved meanders and deltas (see pages 11 and 15) as they reach the sea. Erosion along coastlines forms headlands, bays and spits (see pages 22–25).

These natural arches and stacks on a beach in Spain were created by erosion.

THE WATER CYCLE

Rivers and coasts are both part of the water cycle. Water falls from clouds on to the land as rain, snow, sleet or hail. This water is carried from high ground to low ground by rivers or through underground channels. It ends up in lakes, seas or oceans, where it evaporates into clouds when it is warmed by heat from the Sun, and the cycle begins again.

MAP MASTERS

Rivers and coasts were some of the earliest features recorded on maps. People made maps of rivers and their tributaries (connecting rivers and streams) so that they knew which areas could be accessed inland by boat. Sailors kept records of coastlines to track their voyages and the areas that they had explored.

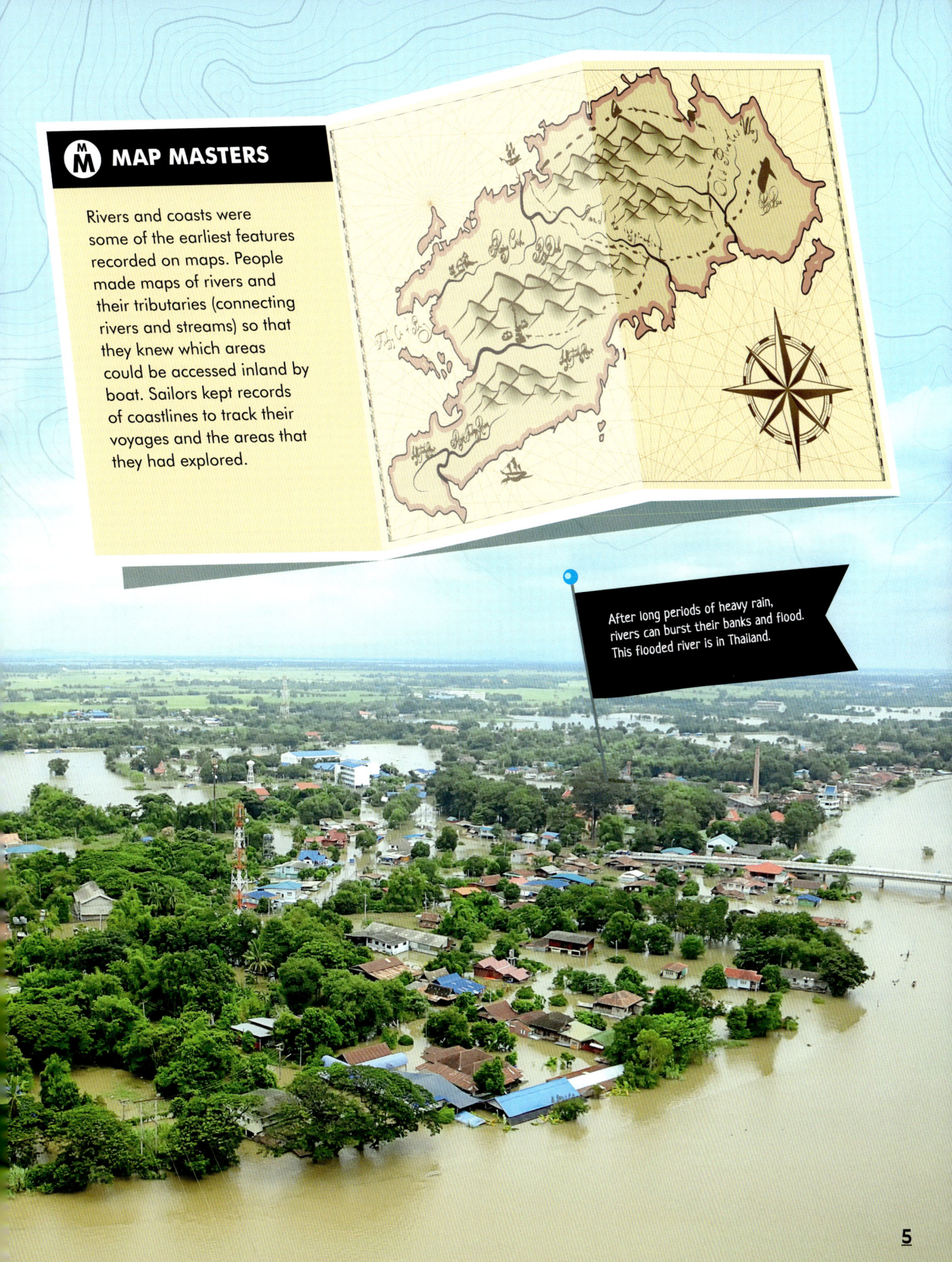

After long periods of heavy rain, rivers can burst their banks and flood. This flooded river is in Thailand.

A RIVER'S SOURCE

The source of a river is where it begins. At its source, a river is just a tiny stream. As it travels away from its source, it grows larger and gains more water.

STARTING HIGH

Most rivers begin high up in the mountains. They form from falling rain, melting snow or ice from glaciers, or where underground water comes to the surface. Some rivers also start from lakes.

Lake Itasca in Minnesota, USA, is the source of the Mississippi River.

Rivers start out narrow close to the source and become wider as they move towards their mouth.

Various tributaries come together to form the Gandaki River in Nepal, which is itself a tributary of the Ganges River in India.

TRIBUTARIES

As a river leaves its source, it is just a tiny stream that flows downhill. Other small streams flow into the river, bringing extra water and making it larger. These streams are known as tributaries. Most rivers have many tributaries of different sizes.

 MAP MASTERS

Early mapmakers were interested in discovering the official source of major rivers. In the past, the furthest point upstream on the tributary that brought most water to the river was often considered the source. However, this wasn't very reliable, as some tributaries carried more water at certain times of year.

More recently, mapmakers have been able to use new technologies, such as satellite imaging, to create maps of rivers and their tributaries. They now tend to consider the furthest point upstream on the longest tributary of the river as the source.

SATELLITE IMAGING

7

MAPPING THE AMAZON RIVER

The Amazon River flows through the north of South America. The Amazon Rainforest, one of the most biodiverse areas on Earth, is located in its basin, which is coloured in yellow on the map below.

MEASUREMENT MYSTERIES

The Amazon River has many tributaries, which has made it hard for geographers to identify its exact source. For this reason, it's also difficult to estimate the precise length of the Amazon River, as no one knows where to start measuring from.

The Amazon River basin, home to the Amazon Rainforest, measures 7 million square km.

VENEZUELA

COLOMBIA

ECUADOR

1 Marañón River

PERU

3 Mantaro River

2 Apurímac River

BOLIVIA

1 THE MARAÑÓN RIVER

In the eighteenth century, geographers believed that the Marañón River contributed the most water to the Amazon. Therefore, its source, Lake Lauricocha, was considered the source of the Amazon.

FACT
The length of the Amazon River is around the same as the distance between New York City and Rome!

8

❷ THE APURÍMAC RIVER

In the twentieth century, the definition of what should be considered a river's source changed (see page 7). Now, it was the furthest point upstream of a river's longest tributary. Geographers identified the Apurímac River as the Amazon's longest tributary.

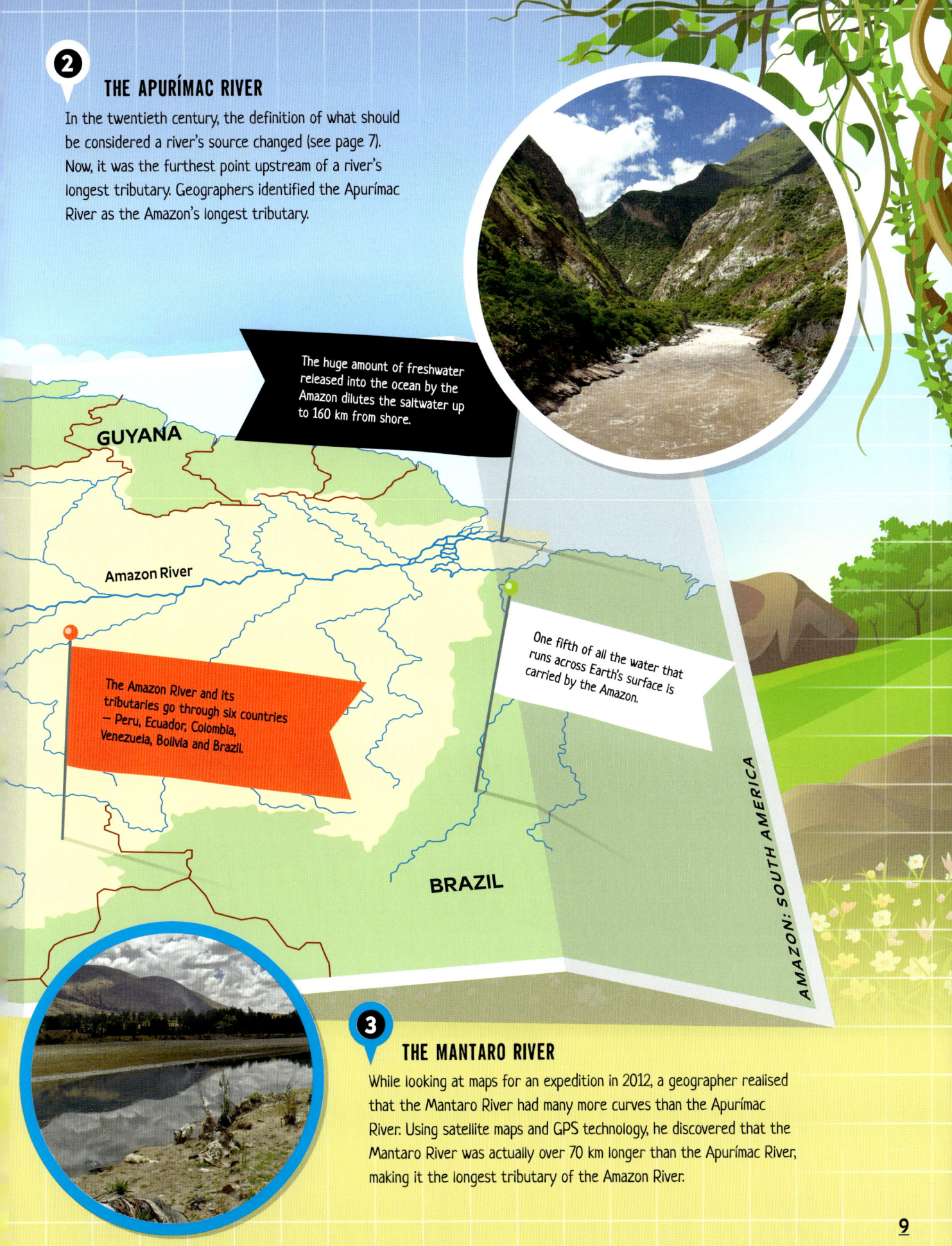

The huge amount of freshwater released into the ocean by the Amazon dilutes the saltwater up to 160 km from shore.

The Amazon River and its tributaries go through six countries — Peru, Ecuador, Colombia, Venezuela, Bolivia and Brazil.

One fifth of all the water that runs across Earth's surface is carried by the Amazon.

❸ THE MANTARO RIVER

While looking at maps for an expedition in 2012, a geographer realised that the Mantaro River had many more curves than the Apurímac River. Using satellite maps and GPS technology, he discovered that the Mantaro River was actually over 70 km longer than the Apurímac River, making it the longest tributary of the Amazon River.

THE UPPER AND MIDDLE COURSES

A river goes through different stages before it reaches its mouth in a lake, sea or ocean. The first two stages are called the upper and middle courses.

CARVING CHANNELS

Rivers move very fast in the upper course because they are travelling down steep slopes. They contain and carry lots of small rocks and sand that erode the riverbed and cut deep channels into the ground. Over time, this creates valleys and gorges. Waterfalls are also common in this part of a river.

The Verdon River has cut a steep gorge into the Alps mountains in France, near its source.

hard rock remains

soft rock is undercut

waterfall

plunge pool

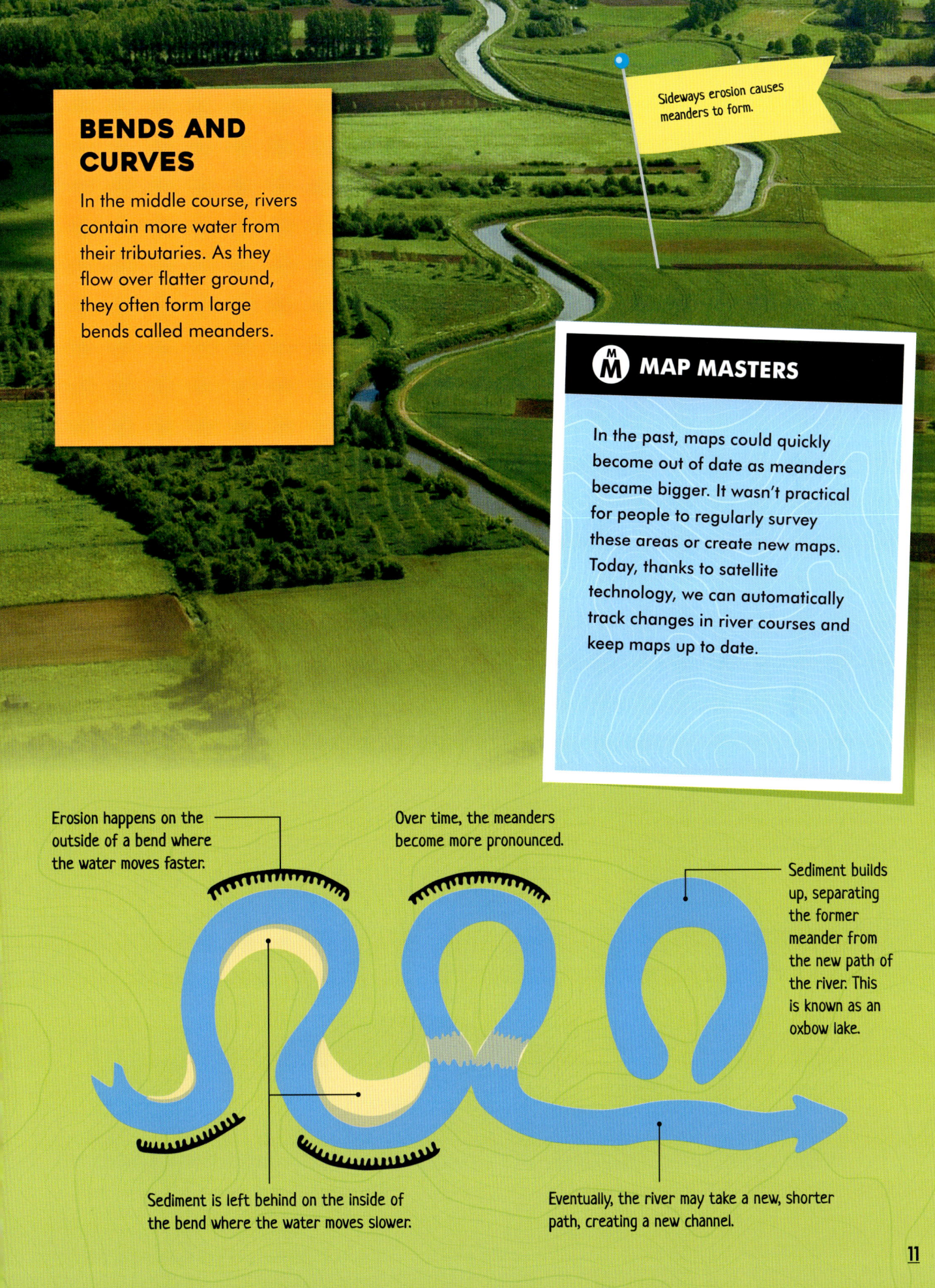

BENDS AND CURVES

In the middle course, rivers contain more water from their tributaries. As they flow over flatter ground, they often form large bends called meanders.

Sideways erosion causes meanders to form.

MAP MASTERS

In the past, maps could quickly become out of date as meanders became bigger. It wasn't practical for people to regularly survey these areas or create new maps. Today, thanks to satellite technology, we can automatically track changes in river courses and keep maps up to date.

Erosion happens on the outside of a bend where the water moves faster.

Over time, the meanders become more pronounced.

Sediment builds up, separating the former meander from the new path of the river. This is known as an oxbow lake.

Sediment is left behind on the inside of the bend where the water moves slower.

Eventually, the river may take a new, shorter path, creating a new channel.

11

MAPPING THE KENTUCKY BEND

The Kentucky Bend is a big bend of the Mississippi River in the USA. The area of land inside the bend belongs to the state of Kentucky, despite being totally cut off from the rest of the state!

STATE SURPRISE

When mapmakers were drawing up the boundaries for some US states in the late eighteenth century, they hadn't actually surveyed much of the area, so they had to estimate where the boundaries should go.

When they eventually came to survey the boundary between Kentucky and Tennessee, they realised that the Kentucky Bend meander cut right through the middle of the state boundary. The mapmakers weren't prepared to change the boundaries, so this small, cut-off area remained part of Kentucky.

The town of New Madrid, Missouri, is located at the top of the Kentucky Bend. It was destroyed in the 1812 earthquake.

temporary waterfalls

2

Kentucky Bend

The Mississippi River is the longest river in North America. It lies entirely within the USA.

MISSOURI

Mississippi River

END OF THE BEND

Eventually, the Mississippi River may cut across the Kentucky Bend as this is a shorter path than going all the way around it. This would create an oxbow lake (see page 11).

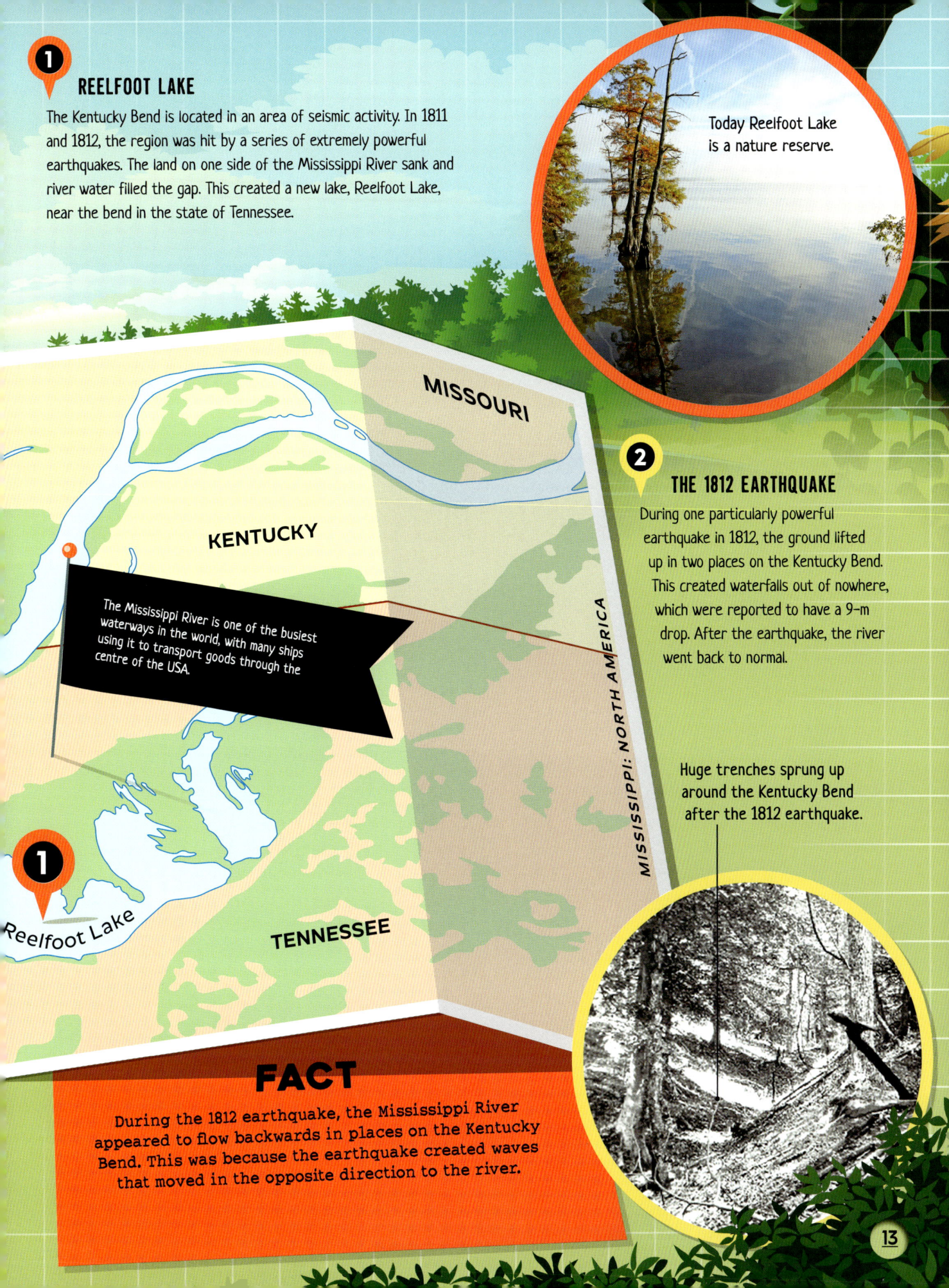

1 REELFOOT LAKE

The Kentucky Bend is located in an area of seismic activity. In 1811 and 1812, the region was hit by a series of extremely powerful earthquakes. The land on one side of the Mississippi River sank and river water filled the gap. This created a new lake, Reelfoot Lake, near the bend in the state of Tennessee.

Today Reelfoot Lake is a nature reserve.

The Mississippi River is one of the busiest waterways in the world, with many ships using it to transport goods through the centre of the USA.

2 THE 1812 EARTHQUAKE

During one particularly powerful earthquake in 1812, the ground lifted up in two places on the Kentucky Bend. This created waterfalls out of nowhere, which were reported to have a 9-m drop. After the earthquake, the river went back to normal.

Huge trenches sprung up around the Kentucky Bend after the 1812 earthquake.

FACT

During the 1812 earthquake, the Mississippi River appeared to flow backwards in places on the Kentucky Bend. This was because the earthquake created waves that moved in the opposite direction to the river.

REACHING THE SEA

As rivers move towards their mouth, they slow down and become much wider and deeper. This stage is known as the lower course.

MUDDY WATERS

In the lower course, tides bring saltwater up into the river where it mixes with freshwater. The river loses energy and slows down, dropping the sediment that it is carrying. The sediment mixes with the water to form mud.

Herons are often seen in water where rivers meet the sea.

Some slow-flowing rivers form estuaries as they meet the sea. These are partially enclosed areas at the mouth of a river.

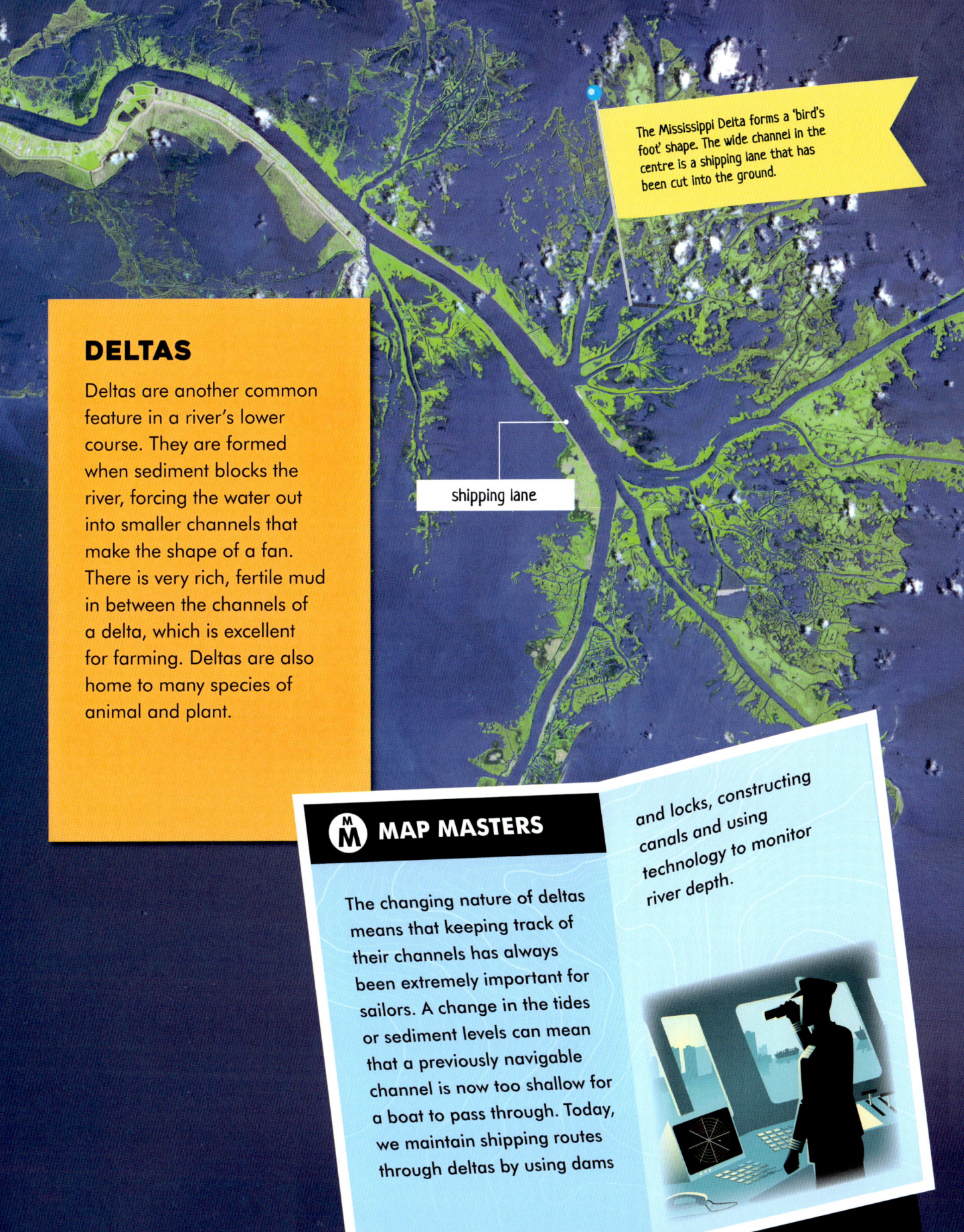

The Mississippi Delta forms a 'bird's foot' shape. The wide channel in the centre is a shipping lane that has been cut into the ground.

shipping lane

DELTAS

Deltas are another common feature in a river's lower course. They are formed when sediment blocks the river, forcing the water out into smaller channels that make the shape of a fan. There is very rich, fertile mud in between the channels of a delta, which is excellent for farming. Deltas are also home to many species of animal and plant.

MAP MASTERS

The changing nature of deltas means that keeping track of their channels has always been extremely important for sailors. A change in the tides or sediment levels can mean that a previously navigable channel is now too shallow for a boat to pass through. Today, we maintain shipping routes through deltas by using dams and locks, constructing canals and using technology to monitor river depth.

MAPPING THE NILE DELTA

The Nile River begins in central Africa and travels north before draining into the Mediterranean Sea through a massive delta, which measures 160 km from north to south.

CHANGING SHAPE

People have lived in the Nile Delta for thousands of years. They kept records of its shape and the position of its channels. This helps geographers to track how the delta has changed shape over time due to natural and artificial causes.

Mediterranean Sea

Rosetta

Alexandria

2

Rosetta branch

More than half of Egypt's crops are grown in the Nile Delta.

Ancient channels
Modern channels

The city of Damietta, Egypt, sits at the mouth of one of the branches of the Nile Delta.

1

DIFFERENT BRANCHES

In the past, the Nile Delta had different main channels. According to the ancient Greek geographer Strabo in the first century CE, there were seven channels. Today, just two main branches remain: the Rosetta branch and the Damietta branch. This is because of natural changes in sediment levels and artificial redirection of the river to try to control flooding.

② ANCIENT FARMING

The area around the Nile Delta once had some of the most fertile soil in Africa. It was a key farming area for the ancient Egyptians who lived in this region. The ancient Egyptians explored and knew the area of the delta well, but didn't explore the upper course of the Nile or its tributaries.

The effect of the Nile (and its previous flooding) can be seen in this image taken by a NASA satellite. The regular flooding of the river created green, fertile land in the middle of the desert.

There are several large lagoons on the coast of the Nile Delta.

① Damietta

Damietta branch

Around 95 million people, 41 per cent of Egypt's population, live in the Nile Delta.

Cairo

Nile River

NILE: EGYPT

THE FUTURE

The construction of the Aswan High Dam in the 1960s and 1970s stopped the Nile from flooding. As a result, 98 per cent less sediment reaches the Nile Delta, meaning less fertile mud can form. In addition, rising sea levels caused by global warming mean that seawater is flooding and covering the delta. In the future, the shape of the delta may change significantly, so it will need to be resurveyed.

FACT

Nearly 3,000 square km (approximately one eighth) of the delta could have sunk by the year 2100 if sea levels continue to rise as a result of global warming, and if Egypt continues to pump water out of the delta for farming, factories and household use.

The Aswan High Dam contains a hydroelectric power plant (see page 27). The plant generates electricity for nearby towns and cities.

TYPES OF **COAST**

Many different types of landscape can be seen along the coast. The coasts are always changing, as the daily rise and fall of the tide covers and uncovers coastal habitats, and carves away new coastal features.

SAND AND PEBBLES

Beaches are formed from sand or pebbles. They are covered by the sea at high tide. At low tide, the water level drops and the beach is left uncovered again. Tides are caused by gravity from the Moon and the Sun pulling on Earth's oceans.

This beach has both sand and larger rocks that have fallen away from the rocky edges of the beach because of erosion from strong waves.

low tide

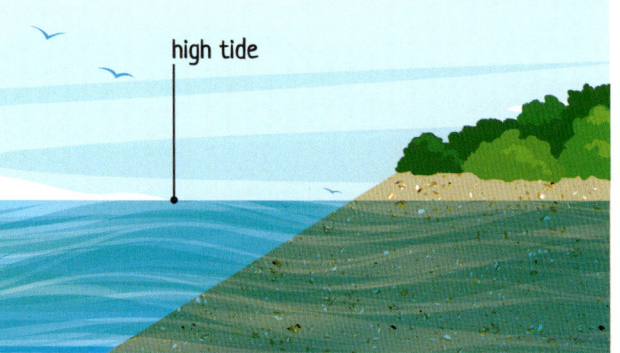

high tide

18

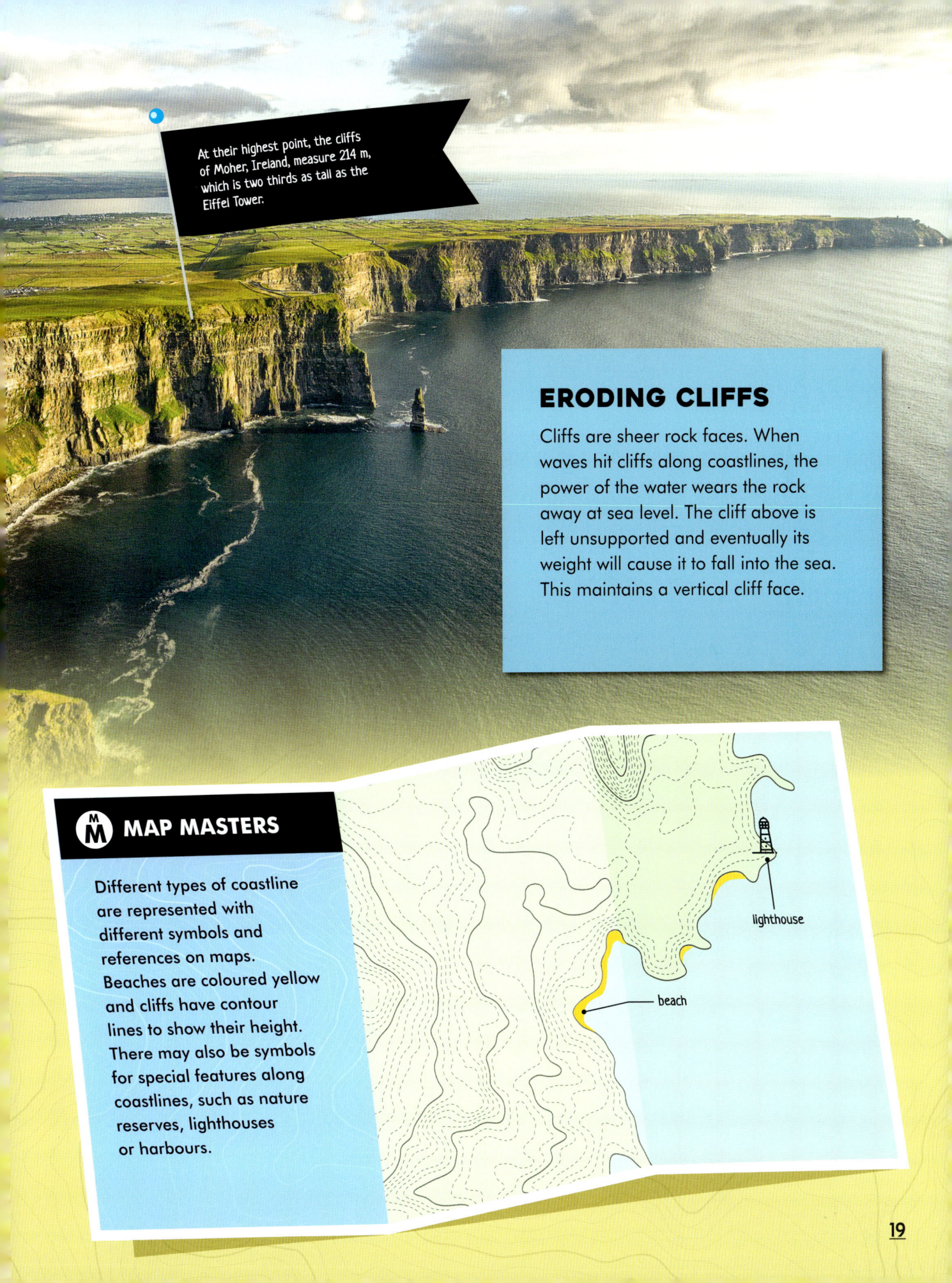

At their highest point, the cliffs of Moher, Ireland, measure 214 m, which is two thirds as tall as the Eiffel Tower.

ERODING CLIFFS

Cliffs are sheer rock faces. When waves hit cliffs along coastlines, the power of the water wears the rock away at sea level. The cliff above is left unsupported and eventually its weight will cause it to fall into the sea. This maintains a vertical cliff face.

MAP MASTERS

Different types of coastline are represented with different symbols and references on maps. Beaches are coloured yellow and cliffs have contour lines to show their height. There may also be symbols for special features along coastlines, such as nature reserves, lighthouses or harbours.

lighthouse

beach

MAPPING NEW SHORES

Maps are a useful historical source, as well as a geographical reference. By studying ancient maps of coastlines, we can learn about exploration patterns from different periods of time.

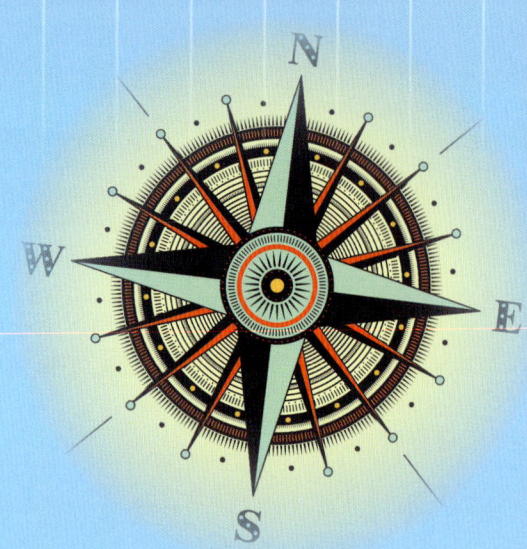

THE DE LA COSA MAP

This is a copy of a map drawn by Juan de la Cosa (c.1450–1510) – a Spanish explorer and mapmaker who accompanied Christopher Columbus on his expeditions to the New World in 1492, 1493 and 1498. His map is one of the earliest documents to show the coastlines of new land surveyed for the first time by Europeans in the Caribbean.

EUROPEAN EXPLORATION

We can use de la Cosa's map to understand which coastlines and areas were known to European sailors. The accuracy of the coastlines of Africa, Europe, the Middle East and the Caribbean islands shows us that these areas had been explored and surveyed. The inaccurate, imagined coastlines of North and South America reveal that these areas were still unknown.

The map was based on observations by de la Cosa and other explorers.

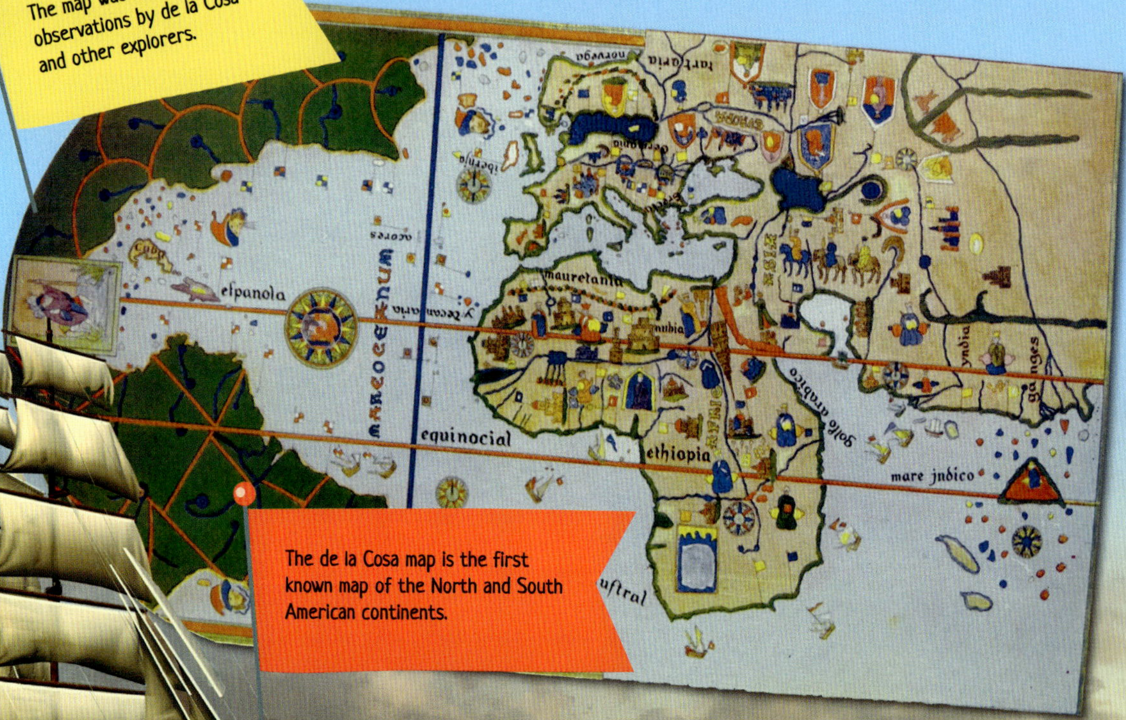

The de la Cosa map is the first known map of the North and South American continents.

FURTHER AFIELD

This map, created by Gerardus Mercator (1512–1594) in 1569, shows us the progress made by European explorers in North and South America. Less than one hundred years after de la Cosa's map was made, sailors had surveyed huge areas of coastline. They reported their findings back to mapmakers in Europe, such as Mercator, who used their notes to create maps.

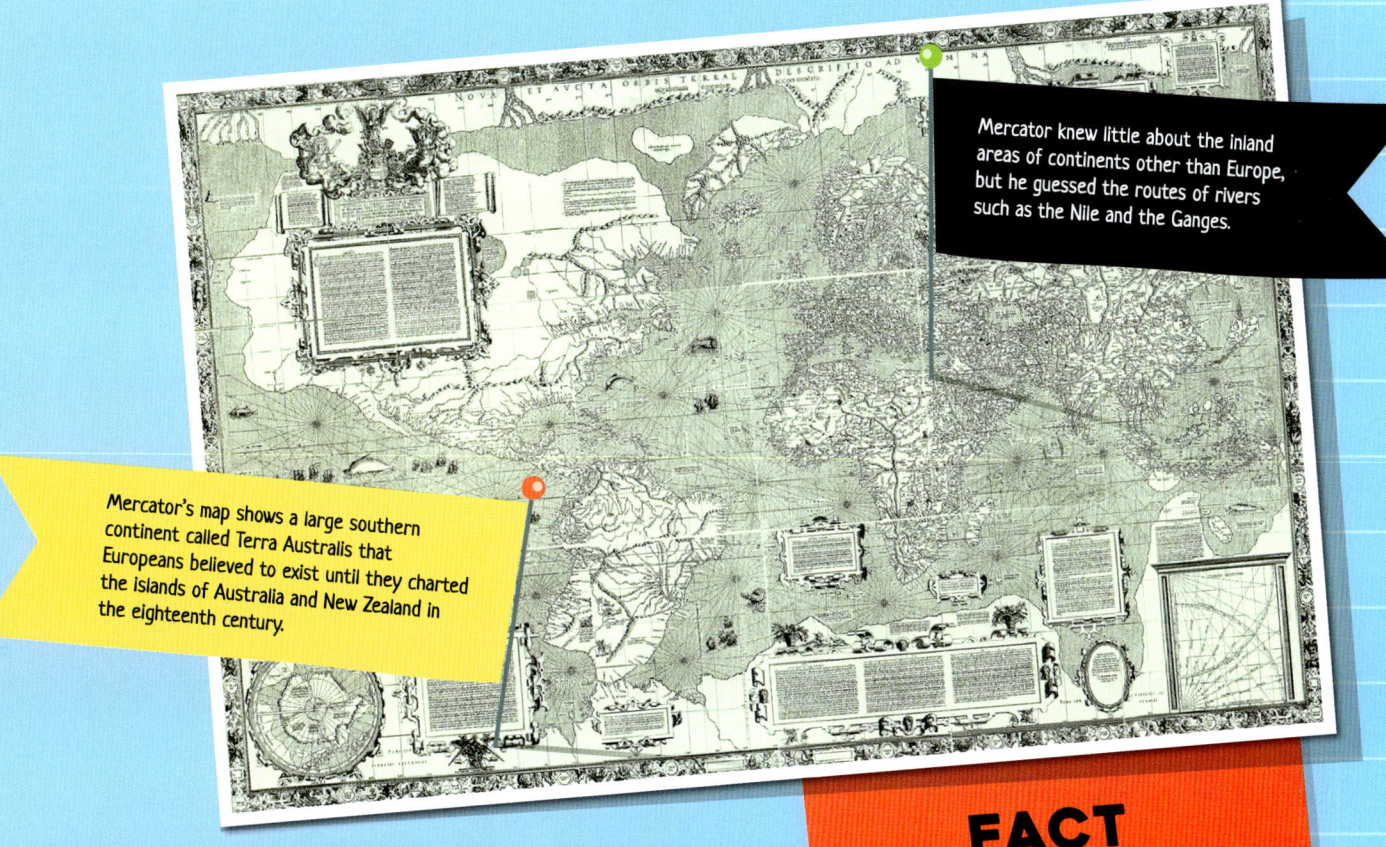

Mercator knew little about the inland areas of continents other than Europe, but he guessed the routes of rivers such as the Nile and the Ganges.

Mercator's map shows a large southern continent called Terra Australis that Europeans believed to exist until they charted the islands of Australia and New Zealand in the eighteenth century.

3D TO 2D

Mercator's map is famous for its projection (way of representing the surface of a globe in a map). As Earth is a 3D sphere, its lines of latitude (north to south) and longitude (east to west) are curved. Before Mercator, many maps were drawn with curved lines of latitude and longitude, which made it hard for sailors to chart a direct, straight course. Mercator's new projection kept lines of latitude and longitude straight. It later became very popular with navigators in the eighteenth century, and was used frequently into the twentieth century.

FACT

Mercator's map has recently been replaced as its projection distorted the size of land at the north and south poles, making it quite inaccurate. For example, Greenland appears to be the same size as Africa, although it only measures 2,166,086 square km, while Africa measures 30,365,000 square km.

GREENLAND
As drawn on Mercator's map

AFRICA
(true size)

GREENLAND

Shown actual size compared to Africa

COASTAL CHANGES

Coasts change over time, both because of erosion from waves wearing away rock, and the build-up of new land from sand carried in water. This leads to unique rock and land formations along the coast.

WEARING AWAY

The force and pressure of waves wears away the rock along coasts. The rock eventually shatters and falls into the water. Soft rocks erode faster than hard rocks. Over time, areas of soft rock wear away to form bays, leaving areas of harder rock sticking out as headlands.

When waves hit the base of tall cliffs, small sections are eroded away and caves form. If a cave breaks through to the other side of a headland, it creates a natural arch.

BUILDING UP

The direction of the wind pushes waves on to the coast at an angle. The water carries sand and pebbles up on the beach at the same angle. However, the wave flows back to the ocean in a straight line. Gradually, this motion moves sand and pebbles along the beach, and can even cause beaches to shift position along a coastline. This process is known as longshore drift.

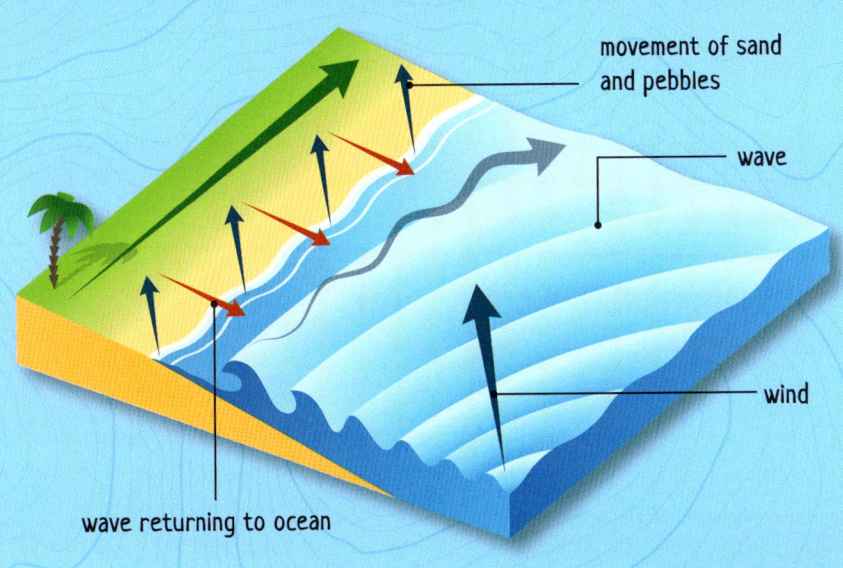

movement of sand and pebbles

wave

wind

wave returning to ocean

MAP MASTERS

Before sailors developed navigational tools to track their route, they had to rely on sight. Near to the coast, they relied on coastal landmarks, such as bays and headlands, to check that they were on course. For longer journeys across open water, they had to depend on the position of the Sun and the stars.

The wind blows loose, dry sand that has washed up on beaches into sand dunes.

23

MAPPING LA MANGA

La Manga is a 22-km-long spit in southeast Spain that blocks off a small lagoon called the Mar Menor. Thanks to ancient records and maps, we are able to track how erosion has changed the spit and the lagoon over time.

FROM BAY TO LAGOON

Originally, this area was a bay with a headland on either side. Over time, sand and sediment carried by ocean waves clumped together with underwater rocks at each of the headlands. Slowly, more sand and sediment built up, creating a long spit that stretched across the whole bay before meeting in the middle.

The beaches along both sides of the spit are heavily built up with hotels, restaurants and shops.

FACT
The largest channel that connects the Mar Menor to the Mediterranean Sea is 80 per cent blocked by sediment. If it were to close completely, the lagoon would eventually dry up entirely, leaving many species without a home.

THE SPIT

The spit varies in width, measuring between 100 m and 1.2 km wide in different places. It contains four main channels that let water flow between the Mar Menor and the Mediterranean Sea.

2 SALT FLATS

The water in the Mar Menor is saltier than most seas and oceans. This is because little water enters the lagoon. When water evaporates from the lagoon, high levels of salt are left behind. Salt flats have formed to the north of the Mar Menor. These are areas where evaporation has removed almost all of the water, leaving behind a layer of salt.

The average depth of the water in the Mar Menor is 3–4 m.

Mar Menor

There are five small islands within the lagoon.

La Manga spit

The Mar Menor is the largest saltwater lagoon in Europe.

Mediterranean Sea

Salt is harvested from the salt flats in the Mar Menor for cooking and other uses.

3 ENVIRONMENTAL ISSUES

Human activity, such as tourism along the coast and watersports in the lagoon, is harming the area around the Mar Menor. As little water is able to escape the lagoon, any polluted water is trapped inside. Pollution from agriculture leads to the build-up of toxic algae, which damages the lagoon's fragile ecosystem.

In 2019, thousands of fish died in the Mar Menor due to lack of oxygen in the water, caused by pollution.

LA MANGA: SPAIN

25

USING WATER

People use water from rivers and coasts in many ways, including for transport, to produce electricity and for general use in our homes and industries.

DRINKING WATER

In many places around the world, people depend on water from rivers for drinking and household use. In areas with little freshwater, saltwater can be turned into freshwater by removing the salt in desalination plants. These plants are built along the coast for easy access to saltwater.

Many items are still transported by ship along rivers and across seas. This is a cheaper form of transporting heavy objects than aeroplane.

HYDROELECTRIC POWER

Moving water can be used to generate electricity in hydroelectric power plants. These are usually built in dams across rivers. The movement of water through the dam turns a turbine, which powers a generator that creates electricity. This electricity is then sent out to homes and businesses along electricity cables.

 MAP MASTERS

Engineers look at maps of rivers when choosing the location of a new hydroelectric dam. They often select the narrowest point of the river, so that the dam can be smaller. They also need to consider the area upstream from the dam, as this will be flooded after the dam is complete. Engineers prefer to use areas with valley walls to contain the extra water, with no settlements or special animal habitats that will be destroyed.

We can also use the movement of the tides to generate electricity. It can be hard to find the right coastal location for tidal power plants, so they are less common than hydroelectric plants.

MAPPING THE THREE GORGES DAM

The Three Gorges Dam is a hydroelectric dam on the Yangtze River in China. The construction of the dam resulted in extensive flooding, creating a huge reservoir and changing the landscape around the dam permanently.

BUILDING THE DAM

The idea of building a dam on the Yangtze River was discussed many times throughout the twentieth century as a way of controlling flooding downstream and generating electricity. However, there were fears about flooding, pollution and the risk of the dam collapsing. Eventually, plans for the dam were approved in 1992 and construction began in 1994. The dam was completed in 2006.

The construction of the Three Gorges Dam dramatically changed the surrounding area.

AFTER

BEFORE

The Yangtze River is the third longest river in the world, measuring 6,300 km.

THE THREE GORGES

The dam is located downriver from the Qutang, Wu and Xiling gorges, also known as the Three Gorges. These are three deep canyons in the middle course of the Yangtze River that are well known for their beautiful scenery. Much of the Three Gorges and other upstream areas, including animal habitats, towns and historical sites, were submerged after the construction of the dam. Large numbers of people had to move away and many fragile ecosystems were destroyed.

The Yangtze River is now much deeper upstream of the dam. This means that large ships can sail along it, which has improved transport links.

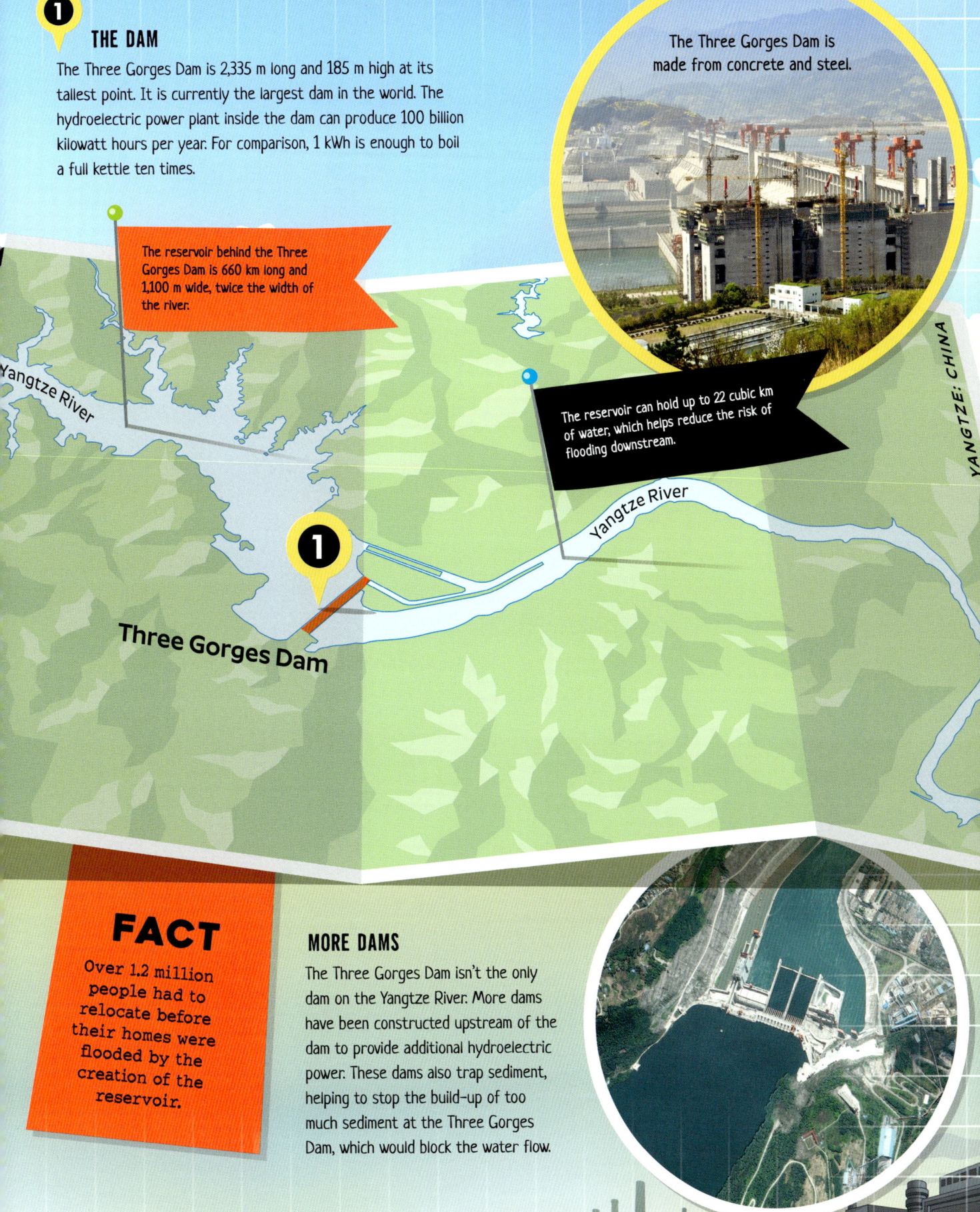

❶ THE DAM

The Three Gorges Dam is 2,335 m long and 185 m high at its tallest point. It is currently the largest dam in the world. The hydroelectric power plant inside the dam can produce 100 billion kilowatt hours per year. For comparison, 1 kWh is enough to boil a full kettle ten times.

The reservoir behind the Three Gorges Dam is 660 km long and 1,100 m wide, twice the width of the river.

The Three Gorges Dam is made from concrete and steel.

The reservoir can hold up to 22 cubic km of water, which helps reduce the risk of flooding downstream.

YANGTZE: CHINA

FACT

Over 1.2 million people had to relocate before their homes were flooded by the creation of the reservoir.

MORE DAMS

The Three Gorges Dam isn't the only dam on the Yangtze River. More dams have been constructed upstream of the dam to provide additional hydroelectric power. These dams also trap sediment, helping to stop the build-up of too much sediment at the Three Gorges Dam, which would block the water flow.

GLOSSARY

basin the area of land from which water drains into a river

bay a part of the coast where the sea is surrounded by land on three sides

boundary a line that marks the edge of something

delta an area of low land where a river splits into several small streams before flowing into the sea

ecosystem all of the living things in an area and the way they affect each other

erode to wear away rock or soil

estuary a partially enclosed area of a river where it meets the sea

evaporate when a liquid heats up and turns into a gas

fertile describes soil that is good to grow plants in

global warming the increase in temperature on Earth caused by the greenhouse effect

headland a piece of land that sticks out into the sea

hydroelectric power plant a power plant that uses the movement of water to generate electricity

inland in the middle of the country, away from the sea

lagoon an area of seawater separated from the sea by a barrier

latitude a position north or south of the equator

longitude a position east or west of an imaginary line between the North and South Poles

meander a bend in a river

navigable deep or wide enough for a boat to pass through

projection a way of representing the surface of a globe in a map

sediment tiny solid pieces in a liquid

seismic related to earthquakes

spit a long, thin beach that goes out into the sea

survey to measure and record the details of an area of land

tributary a river or stream that flows into a larger river

FURTHER INFORMATION

Books

Rivers and Coasts (Fact Planet) by Izzi Howell (Franklin Watts, 2020)

Rivers (Where on Earth?) by Susie Brooks (Wayland, 2017)

Rivers (World Feature Focus) by Rebecca Kahn (Franklin Watts, 2020)

Websites

www.bbc.co.uk/bitesize/topics/z849q6f/articles/z7w8pg8
Find out more about rivers and test your knowledge with a quiz.

www.educationquizzes.com/ks2/geography/coasts
Check your knowledge of coastal features.

www.sciencekids.co.nz/sciencefacts/earth/rivers.html
Discover some fun facts about rivers.

INDEX

Amazon River **8-9**

bays **4, 22, 23, 24**

dams **15, 17, 27, 28-29**
deltas **4, 15, 16-17**

erosion **4, 10, 11, 18, 19, 22, 24**
estuaries **14**

floods **5, 16, 17, 27, 28, 29**
freshwater **4, 9, 14, 26**

headlands **4, 22, 23, 24**
hydroelectric power **17, 27, 28-29**

lakes **4, 6, 8, 10, 13**

meanders **4, 11, 12**
Mississippi River **6, 12-13, 15**

Nile River **16-17, 21**

oceans **4, 9, 10, 18, 23, 24, 25**
oxbow lakes **11, 12**

saltwater **4, 9, 25, 26**
seas **4, 10, 14, 16, 17, 18, 19, 24, 25, 26**
sediment **11, 14, 15, 16, 17, 24, 29**
source **6-7, 8, 9, 10**
spits **4, 24, 25**
streams **5, 6, 7**

Three Gorges Dam **28-29**
tides **14, 15, 18, 27**
tributaries **5, 7, 8, 9, 11, 17**

water cycle **4**
waterfalls **10, 12, 13**